The Theft of America

Samuel Franklin Smith

ISBN: 1548753335
ISBN-13: 978-1548753337

DEDICATION

This book is dedicated to those that work hard but can't get ahead. We hope this short book helps you understand why.

CONTENTS

Samuel Franklin Smith

"Banking was conceived in iniquity and was born in sin. The Bankers own the Earth. Take it away from them, but leave them the power to create deposits, and with the flick of a pen they will create enough deposits to buy it back again. However, take it away from them, and all the fortunes like mine will disappear, and they ought to disappear, for this world would be a happier and better world to live in. But if you wish to remain slaves of the Bankers and pay for the cost of your own slavery, let them continue to create deposits."

Sir Josiah Stamp, President of the Bank of England in the 1920s and the second richest man in Britain at the time.

1

INTRODUCTION

The United States Government is involved in so many wars against other nations, ideologies, and individuals. Have you asked yourself why this is so? Over centuries, wars have been fought for diverse reasons and one of the most important of these reasons is to impose private central banks upon nations. For example, the American revolution was initiated by the actions of King George III of Britain who wanted the colonist to transact business using only currency borrowed from the crown at interest.

"The bank hath benefit of interest on all moneys which it creates out of nothing." -- *William Paterson, founder of the Bank of England in 1694*

To prevent Britain from extorting the people after the revolution, the United States Government implemented its own value based money.

"The refusal of King George 3rd to allow the colonies to operate an honest money system, which freed the ordinary man from the clutches of the money manipulators, was probably the prime cause of the revolution."
-- Benjamin Franklin, Founding Father

Then, the government did its best to keep bankers out of the new government but as it was and is today, bankers are relentless individuals

"Any person holding any office or any stock in any institution in the nature of a bank for issuing or discounting bills or notes payable to bearer or order, cannot be a member of the

House whilst he holds such office or stock." -

- Third Congress of the United States Senate,

23rd of December, 1793, signed by the

President, George Washington

The banking system of any society is very important to the means of subsistence, Mayer Armschel Rothschild was aware of this when he uttered the saying "Let me issue and control a nation's money and I care not who makes the laws". In 1791, the bankers created the First Bank of the United States by an ally of Rothschild, Alexander Hamilton.

After two decades, the charter of the bank expired and the United States Congress refused to renew her charter because of the damaging actions of the bank on the US Economy. Members of the Rothschild family threatened to teach the United States of America a lesson by imploring Britain to go to war against her. The then Prime Minister of Britain, Spencer Perceval who refused was assassinated and his replacement, Robert Banks Jenkinson supported the war.

"If my sons did not want wars, there would be none." -- Gutle Schnaper, wife of Mayer Amschel Rothschild and mother of his five sons

The plan worked., Despite the fact that the

United States won the war provoked by Britain, Congress was forced to grant a charter to another private bank due to the high national debt as a result of the war and as such, the money supply of the country was in private hands again.

The economic problems of unemployment, poverty and high debt as created by the private bank became a huge challenge for the United States until 1832 when Andrew Jackson ran for a second term as President under the slogan "Jackson and no debt". As promised, he was able to stop the approval of a charter for the Second Bank of the United

Sates.

"Gentlemen! I too have been a close observer of the doings of the Bank of the United States. I have had men watching you for a long time, and am convinced that you have used the funds of the bank to speculate in the breadstuffs of the country. When you won, you divided the profits amongst you, and when you lost, you charged it to the bank. You tell me that if I take the deposits from the bank and annul its charter I shall ruin ten thousand families. That may be true, gentlemen, but that is your sin! Should I let you go on, you will ruin fifty thousand families, and that

would be my sin! You are a den of vipers and thieves. I have determined to rout you out, and by the Eternal, (bringing his fist down on the table) I will rout you out!" -- Andrew Jackson, shortly before ending the charter of the Second Bank of the United States. From the original minutes of the Philadelphia committee of citizens sent to meet with President Jackson (February 1834), according to Andrew Jackson and the Bank of the United States (1928) by Stan V. Henkels.

Afterwards, there was an assassination attempt on President Jackson which failed.

Another President of the United States of America after Jackson, Zachary Taylor, also opposed the granting of charter to the private banks and was successfully poisoned and killed. President James Buchanan was also poisoned for opposing the private central bank and was poisoned but he survived while 38 people died.

You may be asking yourself why you are unaware of all this information. The truth is, such information is not helpful to the indoctrination of children to support the corrupt public system and the banking elite so it is being suppressed from public school curricula to prevent you from finding out. This is why you may not know the cause of the civil war.

"The few who understand the system will either be so interested in its profits or be so dependent upon its favors that there will be no opposition from that class, while on the other hand, the great body of people, mentally incapable of comprehending the tremendous advantage that capital derives from the system, will bear its burdens without complaint, and perhaps without even suspecting that the system is inimical to their interests." -The Rothschild brothers of

London writing to associates in New York, 1863

The bankers also approached President Abraham Lincoln on the eve of the Confederacy war to fund the war at 30% interest but the President declined as he saw through their plans to create huge debt for the country. He thereafter issued a national currency, the greenback.

"If this mischievous financial policy, which has its origin in North America, shall become indurated down to a fixture, then that Government will furnish its own money without cost. It will pay off debts and be

without debt. It will have all the money necessary to carry on its commerce. It will become prosperous without precedent in the history of the world. The brains, and wealth of all countries will go to North America. That country must be destroyed or it will destroy every monarchy on the globe." -- The London Times responding to Lincoln's decision to issue government Greenbacks to finance the Civil War, rather than agree to private banker's loans at 30% interest.

The bankers did everything within their powers to oppose President Lincoln. They funded dailies that opposed the greenbacks, sought support from France and Britain against President Lincoln and almost succeeded but were stopped by Russia. After President Lincoln won the war, he wanted to introduce the greenback permanently but was assassinated by a gunshot to the head. After his death, the greenback policy was abolished and the United States went back to money issued by banks at exorbitant interest rates. The Russian Tsar, who assisted Lincoln had multiple attempts on his life as well until he was killed in 1881.

Messrs. Rothschild & Sons to Mr. Sherman.
[Cable message.]

April 12, 1878.

Hon. John Sherman,

Secretary of the Treasury, Washington D. C.:

Very pleased we have entered into relations again with American Government. Shall do our best to make the business successful.

ROTHSCHILDS.

James A. Garfield was elected President in 1880 on a platform of government control of the money supply.

"The chief duty of the National Government in connection with the currency of the

14

country is to coin money and declare its value. Grave doubts have been entertained whether Congress is authorized by the Constitution to make any form of paper money legal tender. The present issue of United States notes has been sustained by the necessities of war; but such paper should depend for its value and currency upon its convenience in use and its prompt redemption in coin at the will of the holder, and not upon its compulsory circulation. These notes are not money, but promises to pay money. If the holders demand it, the promise should be kept. -- James Garfield

"By the experience of commercial nations in all ages it has been found that gold and silver afford the only safe foundation for a monetary system. Confusion has recently been created by variations in the relative value of the two metals, but I confidently believe that arrangements can be made between the leading commercial nations which will secure the general use of both metals. Congress should provide that the compulsory coinage of silver now required by law may not disturb our monetary system by driving either metal out of circulation. If possible, such an adjustment should be made

that the purchasing power of every coined dollar will be exactly equal to its debt-paying power in all the markets of the world. --James Garfield

Over the ensuing decades, any President who opposed the bankers were killed or forced out of office. This continued till the Rothschild family and the Warburgs of Germany (two powerful banking families) met to form the Third Bank of the United States in 1913. The name of the bank was changed to 'Federal Reserve Bank' so as to trick the public into thinking it is a quasi-government institution whereas in reality, it is privately controlled.

In 2012, The Federal Reserve attempted to block Bloomberg News in a Freedom of Information Lawsuit claiming that the Freedom of Information Act did not apply to the trade secrets of the Federal Reserve Bank.

"When you or I write a check, there must be sufficient funds in our account to cover the check; but when the Federal Reserve writes a check, there is no bank deposit on which that check is drawn. When the Federal Reserve writes a check, it is creating money." -- From the Boston Federal Reserve Bank pamphlet, "Putting it Simply."

"Neither paper currency nor deposits have

value as commodities. Intrinsically, a 'dollar' bill is just a piece of paper. Deposits are merely book entries." -- Modern Money Mechanics Workbook - Federal Reserve of Chicago, 1975

"I am afraid the ordinary citizen will not like to be told that the banks can and do create money. And they who control the credit of the nation direct the policy of Governments and hold in the hollow of their hand the destiny of the people." -- Reginald McKenna, as Chairman of the Midland Bank, addressing stockholders in 1924

"States, most especially the large hegemonic

ones, such as the United States and Great Britain, are controlled by the international central banking system, working through secret agreements at the Bank for International Settlements (BIS), and operating through national central banks (such as the Bank of England and the Federal Reserve)... The same international banking cartel that controls the United States today previously controlled Great Britain and held it up as the international hegemon. When the British order faded, and was replaced by the United States, the US ran the global economy. However, the same interests are served. States will be used and discarded at will by the international banking cartel; they are simply tools." -- Andrew Gavin Marshall

2

THE FOUNDATION OF
THE FEDERAL RESERVE

On a cold night in 1910, a coach owned by

Nelson Aldrich, a powerful senator from

Rhode Island left New Jersey at about 10pm.

Aboard the coach were six other people who

would come to define the financial destiny

of the United States of America.

As a very powerful man, Aldrich was very

well-known in Washington DC. Besides

being a senator, he was also the mouthpiece

for big business during that era. As a close

associate of J.P. Morgan, he had extensive

holdings and interest in banking,

manufacturing, and public utilities. His

daughter married John. D. Rockefeller, Jr.

who would later give birth to Nelson

Aldrich Rockefeller who became a Vice

President of the United States.

In the Aldrich coach that night were seven

men whose worth represented about a fourth

of the wealth of the whole world. These men

are:

Nelson W. Aldrich, a Republican senator

and also the "whip", also Chairman of the

National Monetary Commission.

Abraham Piatt Andrew, Assistant Secretary
of the United States Treasury;

Frank A. Vanderlip, president of the
National City Bank of New York, which
was the most powerful bank at the time,
representing William Rockefeller and the
international investment banking house of
Kuhn, Loeb & Company;

Henry P. Davison, an executive and senior
partner of the J.P. Morgan Company;

Charles D. Norton, president of J.P.
Morgan's First National Bank of New York;

Benjamin Strong, head of J.P. Morgan's Bankers Trust Company; and

Paul M. Warburg, a partner in Kuhn, Loeb & Company, representing the interest of the Rothschild of England and France, also brother of Max Warburg who was head of the Warburg banking consortium in Germany and the Netherlands.

This group representing the interest of the wealthiest men at that time journeyed from New Jersey to Georgia under the guise of duck hunting. Their final destination was an island just off the coast of Brunswick, which had recently been bought by J.P. Morgan and some of his associates. This place was known as Jekyll Island, and it was where the theft of American's monetary system started.

The Jekyll Island meeting was meeting arranged to decide on the structure and operation of the takeover of America's banking system by a banking cartel whose goal was to maximize profits and minimize competition between cartel members. In doing so they monopolized the industry and made competition very difficult if not impossible for any new player to come into the field. The idea was to create the structure of what is now a private organization known as the Federal Reserve System.

From the beginning, the Federal Reserve system was a cartel designed to steal the wealth of nations. Let's define a what is a cartel so there is no confusion on the fitting title for this group. A cartel is a group of independent businesses joining together to coordinate the production, pricing, or marketing of their members. The function of a cartel is to eliminate competition in order to increase profitability. This can be done by creating a shared monopoly over their industry, thereby forcing the public to pay higher amounts of money for their goods or services than would be the case if it were under free-enterprise competition.

At the Jekyll Island meeting were representatives of the biggest banking groups in the world at the time: Morgan, Rockefeller, Rothschild, Warburg, and Kuhn Loeb. They often competed with one another, but on this occasion, they were united in their desire to overcome an enemy that is common to all of them—competition.

The desire to eliminate competition at the time was understandable as the banking industry was growing rapidly. Around the time of this meeting in 1910, banks were springing up everywhere. By 1910, there was double the number of banks than there were in 1900. The majority of these banks were setting up shops in the South and West causing the banks in New York to lose its share of the market.

Thirty years earlier, almost all the banks in the US were national banks meaning that they were chartered by the federal government. As a result of this, these banks were located in the major cities and the law permitted them to issue their own currency in the form of bank notes.

By early 1896, the number of banks that are non-national had grown significantly to about 61% and were accountable for 54% of the total banking deposits of the whole country. By 1913 when the Federal Reserve act was passed, the number of non-national banks had already risen to 71% accounting for 57% of total deposits. For the big players at Jekyll Island, this was something they wanted to stamp out as a free market system was a system that limited their profits and power.

There was also a new trend in the industry as banks were financing future growth from profits instead of borrowed capital. This was the result of free-market interest rates which create a realistic balance between debts and thrift. The rates were significantly low enough to attract serious borrowers who are sure of the profitability of their business and their ability to pay but also high enough to repel anyone with the intention of taking loans for frivolous ventures or people who had alternative sources of funding, for example, one's capital.

This balance between debt and thrift was caused by a limited money supply. Banks were able to make loans bigger than their actual deposits available, although there was a limit that was determined by the supply of gold they had.

As a result of this, between 1900 and 1910, seventy percent of the funding responsible for the growth of American companies were generated internally, therefore making many industries dependent on banks. Even the federal government was making a profit. The government had a growing storage of gold which it was using to redeem the dollar (which had been issued during the Civil War) and reducing the national debt. But the Jekyll Island group needed that trend to stop.

The group and also many businessmen wanted to intervene in the free market and upset the balance so that debt can be favored over profit. For this to be done, the supply of money needed to be disconnected from gold and made more abundant, or in their words, elastic.

Normally, when a bank accepts the deposits of a customer, they will give him a "balance". This is a way of saying that they will pay back whatever is deposited at any time the customer needs it. Also, when a customer borrows money from the bank, he is also given a balance which is withdrawn immediately to fulfill the purpose of the loan. Now this arrangement is a ticking time bomb because it means that the bank has made promises to pay more money on demand than it actually has in the vault. Even though the customer who has deposited thinks he can get his money back at any time he wishes, in reality, that money has been given to someone else as a loan and is no longer available at the bank vault. This arrangement is even made more dangerous when banks are allowed to give as loans more money than they collected as deposits. Now if you take into account the fact that the bank uses depositors' money to make other long-term investment, then things can really get scary.

But inasmuch as a small number of depositors ask for their money at one point in time, then everything is good, everyone can smile. But if the public should have any reason to have their confidence shaken and if a large number of people at any point in time should attempt to withdraw their funds, the scheme will be exposed as the bank will not be able to keep its promises and thus is forced to shut down. Then bankruptcy happens.

The same end result could happen (and actually often did before the Federal Reserve System) even if depositors don't make a run on the bank. So instead of withdrawing their funds from the bank at the window of the teller, a customer can simply write a check to buy a good or pay for a service. Now the people selling such goods and service can take the check to a bank for deposit. If that bank is the same as the one from which the check was drawn, then there is no cause for alarm, since there won't be a need to take any real money from the bank's vault. But if the recipient of the check took it to another bank, it will have to be quickly passed to the issuing bank and the two banks will arrange the settlement. However, this is a two-way street. While Bank A is demanding payment from Bank B, Bank B is also clearing checks and demanding payment from Bank A. Therefore, inasmuch as the money continues to flow both ways, there is no issues. But if the flow is not equal, then one of the banks will have to make up the difference by sending money. And if this amount of money required goes over the the bank's total deposits, it could create the same effect as that of run on the bank by depositors.

This demand of money by other banks instead of depositors is what is known as currency drain.

In 1910, currency drain was one of the most common reasons banks were declaring bankruptcy since the banks were following a loan policy that was more reckless than their competitors. As more money was demanded, more money had to be loaned out. Banks were loaning ninety percent of their customers' savings, which at the time was OK. But many banks were pushing this percentage higher in order to get more profit and patronage. After all, the way a bank can make money is through the collection of

interest. And you can't collect interest

without issuing out loans. The more loans

issued, the better. Therefore, many reckless

banks started to "loan up" which means they

are pushing down their reserve ratio. The

reserve ratio is the portion or percentage of

total deposits that banks must have on hand

in cash.

Now, if all banks are forced to issue loans in

the same reserve ratio with other banks,

then, regardless of how small the ratio was,

the amount of checks that needs to be

cleared between them would be balanced.

This means that no serious currency drain could happen.

Of course, the banking industry may fall like a house of cards but the individual banks will not, especially those that are part of a cartel. They would all operate with the same ratio no matter how close it was to the tipping point. This means that under such a uniform operation, no individual bank will get the boot for not meeting its obligations. Failure to meet obligations could be passed to the "economy", "government policy", "interest rates", "trade deficits", "exchange rate of the dollar, or even "capitalism". As of 1910 this idea had not been manifested.

If Bank A started to loan out a bigger percentage of its deposits than its competitors and thus have a smaller reserve ratio than other banks, then it will also have to deal with a huge amount of checks. This means a bank with a very reckless spending policy will need to draw against its reserves in order to make payments to another one which is more conservative and, when it is unable to draw more funds, it will be forced to declare bankruptcy. The financial panics of 1873, 1884, 1893, and 1907 were triggered by currency drains that happened when banks began to loan up in the periods of relative prosperity. In other words, people panicked not because the economy was bad but because the banks had given out so much in loans that they had almost nothing left in the reserves. The banking system failed because the banks were weak not because the system itself was weak.

This was another problem that made the Jekyll Island team come together. Despite the fact that they were all competitors, they were all united against the panic. Therefore, they needed to create a system that enabled them to continue making more pay-on-demand promises than they could keep. For this to happen, they had to force other banks to operate in the same manner, so when disaster happens, blame will be shifted to the national economy instead of themselves.

By making it look like it is not their action but that of the economy, they could get access to tax money and use this money to pay off debts incurred instead of their own funds. The bank bailout of 2008 is a perfect example of such a situation.

So, the Jekyll Island conspirators gathered together to solve the following challenges facing them:

1. How to prevent the growth of small, rival banks to ensure that they get control over the nation's financial resources;

2. How to make the supply of money more elastic so that the trend of private capital formation can be reversed in order to recapture the industrial loan market;

3. How to pool together the reserve of the nation's banks into one large reserve so that all the banks will be inspired to follow the same loan-to-deposit ratios. This will insure some of them from currency drains and bank runs;

In the event that the banking system collapses, the losses can be shifted from the bank owners to the taxpayers.

Everyone present at the meeting knew that

the only way to actualize some of these

plans would be to setup a cartel mechanism

that is similar in operation to that in Europe.

Like all cartels, it had to be created by

legislation and backed by government

powers under the cover of protecting

consumers.

But the problem was how to sell the idea to

the Congress and convince the American

people that the measures were to protect

them. It was a very delicate task. Americans

do not like the idea of a cartel. They don't

like the idea that some business enterprise

will join together to fix prices and prevent competition. It was alien to the free-enterprise system which they enjoy. Voters won't like it. But what if the word "cartel" was not used? What if a more neutral or even attractive name was used to shield this intention? Then this means that the battle would be half-won.

The first step was to follow in the footsteps of the practice in Europe. From that moment onwards, the cartel would operate as a central bank. But that would be only a generic expression. For the purpose of public consumption and legislation, they would create a name that will depict the image of the federal government itself and avoid the word "bank". Furthermore, to create the impression that concentration of power does not exist, regional branches of the cartel would be established and that would be used as a selling point.

Because they were modelling after the European cartel, no other person in the room was more qualified to lead the discussion than Paul Warburg. A quick study of the Federal Reserve System will show that Warburg was its spearhead. In fact, some call him the father of the system.

For a long time, we have all been lied to that the Federal Reserve was created to stabilize the American Economy. A popular textbook on the subject explains that:

"It sprang from the panic of 1907, with its alarming epidemic of bank failures: the country was fed up once and for all with the anarchy of unstable private banking."

But anyone who has studied a little bit of history will know that the Federal Reserve presided over the crash of 1921 and 1929; the Great Depression of 1929 to 1939; the recessions of 1953, 1957, 1969, and 1981; a stock market "Black Monday" in 1987; and inflation of 1000% which killed off 90% of the purchasing power of the US dollar since the Federal Reserve was first created in 1913. By 1990, an American will need $10,000 to buy only what cost $1000 in 1914. But that great loss in value of the dollar was not absorbed by the bank operators. No, it was quietly transferred to the Federal Government under the guise of hidden and insidious taxation. The Federal Reserve System was the vehicle for this achievement.

But according to Newton's third law of motion: action and reaction are equal and opposite. That is to say, every action leads to a consequence. The confiscation of wealth using the Federal Reserve System has brought on the American people a grave consequence. We are now experiencing increasing corporate and personal debts and increasing personal and corporate bankruptcies. Interest on national debts is taking away a very large chunk of our tax money. Local industries are being replaced by overseas competition even as we face international trade deficits, with many states managing to stay above economic recession.

3

THE CONTROVERSIAL
FEDERAL RESERVE

The passage of the Federal Reserve Act was extremely controversial in nature. On the day it was passed by Congress in 1913, members of Congress who opposed it were absent and President Woodrow Wilson who signed it into law later claimed he regretted his actions.

The vote in Congress occurred during Christmas recess and only 6 congressmen were physically present when they enacted it. Hardly a majority or what is also called a "proper quorum". They were obviously there to "take one for the rest of the team" in case a public backlash occurred.

"People who will not turn a shovel full of dirt on the project nor contribute a pound of material, will collect more money from the United States than will the People who supply all the material and do all the work. This is the terrible thing about interest ...But here is the point: If the Nation can issue a dollar

bond it can issue a dollar bill. The element that makes the bond good makes the bill good also. The difference between the bond and the bill is that the bond lets the money broker collect twice the amount of the bond and an additional 20%. Whereas the currency, the honest sort provided by the Constitution pays nobody but those who contribute in some useful way. It is absurd to say our Country can issue bonds and cannot issue currency. Both are promises to pay, but one fattens the usurer and the other helps the People. If the currency issued by the People were no good, then the bonds would be no good, either. It is a terrible situation when the Government, to insure the National Wealth, must go in debt and submit to ruinous interest charges at the hands of men who control the fictitious value of gold." -- Thomas A. Edison

In 1914, The First World War began. The reality is that while Germany was not the initial focus, she became a 'person of interest' when Britain saw Germany as an economic threat. At the time, Germany was run by a government managed Central Bank that steadied inflation and managed unemployment. After the war, Germany was forced to pay the three times the cost of the war to each participating country which plunged the country into debt. Despite all these odds, the National Socialists which took over from the Weimer Republic issued their own state currency which was free from interest as it was not borrowed from the private bankers. Germany quickly began to rebuild her economy and succeeded which was referred to as the 'German Miracle' by the media.

Germany's resurgence angered the private bankers and Great Britain who started making moves as early as 1933 to organize a global boycott against Germany. While

Adolf Hitler was a despotic, evil leader, other powerful nations could have ousted him without causing a war. The war was a means of grounding Germany's resurging economy.

*"Should Germany merchandise (do business) again in the next 50 years we have led this war (WW1) in vain." - **Winston Churchill in The Times (1919)***

*"We will force this war upon Hitler, if he wants it or not." - **Winston Churchill (1936 broadcast)***

*"Germany becomes too powerful. We have to crush it." - **Winston Churchill** (November*

1936 speaking to US - General Robert E. Wood)

"This war is an English war and its goal is the destruction of Germany." - **Winston Churchill (-** *Autumn 1939 broadcast)*

"The war wasn't only about abolishing fascism, but to conquer sales markets. We could have, if we had intended so, prevented this war from breaking out without doing one shot, but we didn't want to."- **Winston Churchill to Truman (Fultun, USA March 1946)**

"Germany's unforgivable crime before WW2

was its attempt to loosen its economy out of the world trade system and to build up an independent exchange system from which the world-finance couldn't profit anymore. ...We butchered the wrong pig." **-Winston Churchill (The Second World War - Bern, 1960)**

President Franklin Roosevelt who initiated the New Deal Act to stimulate America's economy after the global depression of the 1920s was also targeted because his economic plan would restructure and redistribute wealth to create a higher standard of living for the average American. Of course, the Private bankers opposed it as it would push them away from the top of the food chain. Marine Major General Smedley Butler was approached by the private banking group to lead a coup against President Roosevelt that would crush social unrest and be answerable to the private bankers rather than the people. The honorable General pretended to play along but informed Congress of the plan. Congress failed to act as it was in the pocket of the private bankers. President Roosevelt was threatened with artificial economic challenges and as such, could not act. The minutes of Congressional hearing as regards the coup was declassified in 1967. Roosevelt was finally able to punish the Coup plotters during World War II.

"I spent 33 years and four months in active military service as a member of our country's most agile military force -- the Marine Corps. I served in all commissioned ranks from second lieutenant to Major General. And during that period I spent more of my time being a high--class muscle man for Big Business, for Wall Street and for the bankers. In short, I was a racketeer, a gangster for capitalism. I suspected I was just a part of a racket at the time. Now I am sure of it. Like

all members of the military profession I never had an original thought until I left the service. My mental faculties remained in suspended animation while I obeyed the orders of the higher-ups. This is typical with everyone in the military service. Thus I helped make Mexico and especially Tampico safe for American oil interests in 1914. I helped make Haiti and Cuba a decent place for the National City Bank boys to collect revenues in. I helped in the raping of half a dozen Central American republics for the benefit of Wall Street. The record of racketeering is long. I helped purify

Nicaragua for the international banking house of Brown Brothers in 1909-12. I brought light to the Dominican Republic for American sugar interests in 1916. In China in 1927 I helped see to it that the Standard Oil went its way unmolested. During those years, I had, as the boys in the back room would say, a swell racket. I was rewarded with honors, medals and promotion. Looking back on it, I feel I might have given Al Capone a few hints. The best he could do was to operate his racket in three city districts. I operated on three continents." -- **General Smedley Butler, former US Marine Corps**

Commandant, 1935

President Kennedy who knew the evils of private bankers signed Executive Order 11110 which ordered the US Treasury to print the government owned US Note. The notes were not borrowed or funded by the private bankers and as such, no one had any obligation to them. He was assassinated five months later and the circulation of the US Notes came to an abrupt end. Today, only a few collectors have those notes. John McCloy, one of the private bankers, was named in the Warren Commission probably to hide the involvement of private bankers in the assassination.

4

HOW THE FEDERAL RESERVE HARMS THE AMERICAN PEOPLE

The best way to explain how this works is

by making an analogy out of a game. First of

all, in a game such as football, there are

certain plays that need to be repeated over

and over again with just a small variation to

suit the special circumstances. Secondly,

there are some set of rules that the players have to follow to ensure that they achieve their aims. Thirdly, the game has an objective and this is at the heart of every player. Lastly, if the spectators don't know the objectives nor understand the rules, they will not be able to comprehend what is going on; this is the state of the Federal Reserve System and the American people.

Now, this game that we are all playing is what is called Bailout. As it has been earlier mentioned, the objective of the game is to shift the inevitable loss from the owners of these big banks to taxpayers; the American people. This is called socializing the risk and privatizing the gain.

This is how that is done. The Federal Reserve System enables commercial banks to make checkbook money out of nothing. They are permitted to loan ten times the amount of money they have on hand or 90% of amounts on deposit, if the reserve ratio is 10%. The banks then derive profit not by spending this legally counterfeited money but by lending it to others and receiving interest on it. When this loan is given out, it is shown in the banker's books as asset because interest is generated on it and the principal will be paid back one day. At the same time, another entry is made at the other side of the checkbook—the liability side. This is because this checkbook money is now in circulation, and most of it will end up in some other banks which will return the canceled checks to the issuing bank for payment. Some people will also bring some of this checkbook money to the bank and ask for real cash.

The issuing bank therefore has a potential money payout liability that is equal to the amount of the loan asset. When a borrower is unable to pay back the loan and there are no assets to compensate for this, the bank will have to write off such a loan as a loss. Now, since most of the money were made from nothing and actually cost the bank nothing except the overhead cost of bookkeeping, nothing really tangible is lost. It is nothing more than a bookkeeping entry.

A bookkeeping loss can also be a bit harmful because it makes the loan to be removed from the ledger as an asset without a reduction in liabilities. Now, this difference has to be made up for through the equity of the owners of the bank. That is a roundabout way of saying that the loan asset may be removed but the money liability still remains. The original checkbook money is still in circulation even though the borrowers of the loan cannot repay it and the issuing bank still has the duty and obligation of redeeming these checks. This means that the only way to balance the books once again is to take from the capital invested by the stockholders of the bank or remove this loss from the current profit of the bank. In any case, the owners of the bank will still lose an amount that is equal to the value of the loan that is defaulted. So, for them, the loss is actually real. If the bank is forced to write off such a large amount of bad loans, it could eventually exceed the total value of the equity of the owners. And when that happens, it means the game is over for them and the bank then collapses into insolvency.

Now, this situation is sufficient enough to make most bankers conservative about their loan policy, which most of them actually do when dealing with individuals and small businesses. But with the Federal Reserve System, the Federal Deposit Insurance Corporation (F.D.I.C.), and the Federal Deposit Loan Corporation (F.D.L.C.), massive loans can now be guaranteed to large corporations and to other governments,

and in the event that these borrowers default

on their loans, the responsibility does not

fall entirely upon them but the taxpayers too.

But they will do this under the explanation

that if those bank or corporations are

allowed to fail, the country will suffer from

unemployment and economic disruption.

The result of this policy is that these banks

have little reason to be cautious in their

actions since they are protected against the

results of their own indiscretion.

The bigger the loan, the better it is for the

owners of these banks because big loans equal big interests and consequently, big profits. A huge loan to the government of a developing country in the order of millions of dollars in annual interest is evidently more profitable than that to a local American business who need jut $50,000 to fund his business. If the interest is paid by this government, then it is party time, but if this country defaults, then the federal government will step in to "protect the public" and use different mechanisms to ensure that the bank continues to receive its interest so that "unemployment does not rise in the country".

The individual and the small businessman find it very difficult to borrow money from these banks at a very reasonable rate because the banks can make more money loaning out money to giant corporations and foreign governments. Also, the bigger the loans, the safer it is for these banks because the government will still ensure that they get their interest back even if the borrowers default. For small loans to individuals, however, there are no such guarantees. Many people will not believe that bailing out the little individual is also important to "saving the system" too. The dollar amount is very small. Therefore, it is only when the amount is far too big that the ploy becomes plausible.

At this point, it is important to note that banks typically don't like to have their loans repaid, except of course to show another borrower that they are dependable. They make their profit from interest paid on the loan, not the repayment of the loan. If a loan is repaid, then the bank just needs to find another borrower that will be an expensive nuisance. It is far better to have the existing borrower pay only the interest and never make payments on the loan itself. This is what is called rolling over the debt and it is one of the reasons banks prefer lending to the government since they don't expect the loan to ever be repaid.

To see why this is true, it is important to understand some basics about government borrowing. The first of this is that there are only a very few cases of government—any government for that matter—actually getting out of debt. For sure, in an era where government is owing over $100 billion, no one lending money to the government by buying Treasury bill expects the government to pay back at maturity except the government sells a new bill of like amount.

Since the system makes it possible for banks to issue out large, unsound loans, it is exactly the kind of loans banks will issue. Furthermore, it is very predictable that bad loans will at the end of the day go into default. When the borrower finally defaults and declares that he cannot pay, then the bank makes the decision to roll over the loan. The bank handles this as if it is a concession, but, in reality, it is a direct move towards their objective of getting perpetual interest. In the end, the borrower comes to the point where he cannot pay the interest again, and that's when everything becomes a bit more complex.

The bank does not want to lose this interest because that is its oxygen. The bank cannot afford, however to let the borrower go into default either. This is because it would require that a write-off which, in turn, could take up all the equities of the owners and put the bank out of business. Therefore, the bank's next move will be to create additional money out of nothing and lend that to the borrower so that he will have enough money to continue to paying that

interest which by now must be paid on the

original loan and the additional loan as well.

What everyone thought would be a disaster

now turns into something extremely

brilliant. This not only maintains the old

loan in the checkbook as an asset, but also

ensures that the bank gets higher interest

payment, thus bigger profit for the bank.

Quite a Ponzi scheme, huh?

Sooner or later, though, the borrower gets

fed up with everything. He is no longer

interested in paying so much money for

interests while having nothing left for himself. Soon, he realizes that he is just working for the usurious bank and, once again he stops paying interest. Now the bank seeing that its lifeblood is threatened huffs and puffs but the borrower cannot simply pay. The bank threatens to take steps that will ensure that the borrower is never able to borrow a loan again. Finally, both parties come to the table and agree on a compromise. Like in the beginning, the bank then creates more money out of nothing and lends it to the borrower to cover the interest on the two loans, but this time, they take it up a notch to provide additional money for

the borrower to have enough to spend on

something else besides interest. This is

where things get further interesting.

Suddenly, the borrower has a very fresh

supply of money for his purpose even after

he has paid off his worrisome interest. The

bank is also happy because it now has a

larger asset, higher interest income, and

even bigger profit. Isn't that just exciting?

Now the previous play can be repeated for

as long as possible until the borrower starts

to realize that he is sinking deeper into debt

every day and the opportunity of getting out

is dimmer and dimmer with each interest

payment. This realization usually comes

when the payment on interest becomes so

large that they now stand toe-to-toe with

their total corporate earnings or the

country's total tax base. This time around

default seems inevitable as roll-overs with

larger loans are rejected.

But wait! There seems to be one more play.

Rescheduling!

The bank agrees to reschedule the loan. This

means the loan will be paid at a lower

interest rate but over a longer period of time.
The strategy is merely cosmetic because it
reduces the monthly payment but extends
the period further. The burden is a little
easier to carry but paying back the capital is
even more unlikely. The day of reckoning is
postponed for the borrower, but the bank
still continues to turn the loan into a
snowballing asset with interest payments.

Finally, the day of reckoning comes. The
borrower's eyes further open to the fact that
he can never repay the capital and later
refuses to pay interest on it. This time,

nothing can be done, except for the final move. The move to bring in the public into the slaughterhouse to "protect them".

Before we continue, it is important to understand that most banks with "problem loans" are still usually profitable. Except for third-world loans, losses due to bad loans to multinational corporations and some developed countries can be absorbed. But the banks won't do that because that will mean a very huge loss to the stockholders since they will be receiving little or no dividends during the adjustment period, and any CEO who decides to take such a course will soon be out of a job at the speed of thought.

This is evident in the fact that while banks have been known to absorb a small portion of the debts to Latin American countries, they continue to give out huge loans to governments of the poorer countries of Africa, Asia, and Eastern Europe. The most important reason is that loans to these poorer countries can still be reactivated to bring in steady streams of income.

How is this possible?

The head of the lending bank and the chief

finance officer of the defaulting corporation or government will form a team and approach the US congress. They will explain that the borrower has exhausted his ability to service the loan and without assistance from the US government, there will be catastrophe for the American people. Not only will there be serious hardship for the American people at home due to job losses, there will also be a serious disruption in the world market. And because of the fact that we are very dependent on those markets, our exports will shrink, foreign capital will emaciate, and Americans will suffer terribly.

They will tell Congress that what they need is for Congress to provide money to the borrower, either directly or indirectly, to allow him to continue to pay the interest on the loan and to put in place new spending programs that will be so profitable that the borrower will be able to pay everyone back.

As part of this proposal, the borrower will agree to accept the direction of a third-party referee in adopting an austerity measure that will ensure that this money to be provided by the Congress will not be wasted. The bank on its own part will also agree to write off a small part of the loan as a sign that it is also willing to share a part of the burden.

This strategy of course is something that has

been orchestrated from the beginning and is

just a step back to make a giant leap in

future profit for the bank. After all the

amount to be lost was created out of nothing

in the first place, and without approaching

the Congress, it will be lost anyway.

Besides, this modest write-off will be made

back when the income stream is restored.

One of the features of this final move is that

the government does not always need to

directly provide the funds. Sometimes, what

it needs to do is provide credit for the funds. This means that future payment is still guaranteed should the borrower default again. Once the US Congress agrees to this proposal, it becomes the co-signer to the loan and eventually the losses are taken from the cashbook of the bank and placed into the heads of the American taxpayers. Money now begins to flow into the banks through a network of agencies, international agencies, foreign aid, and direct subsidies. Congress takes taxpayer money and gives it to these borrowers who then use it to service their loans to the banks.

The Theft of America

5

HISTORICAL EXAMPLES OF HOW THE FEDERAL RESERVE HARMS THE AMERICAN PEOPLE

LOCKHEED

In 1970, Lockheed, the biggest defense

contractor of the Federal Government was at

the edge of bankruptcy. The giant

corporation had borrowed $400 million from the Bank of America and other smaller banks. Because the banks cannot afford to lose a huge source of income stream from this loan and the fact that they do not want to see such a huge asset disappear from their ledgers, they decided in typical fashion to use the weapon they have fashioned in cases like these. The banks, together with the management of Lockheed, its stakeholders, labor unions descended as lobbyists on Washington, D.C. Many politicians were told that if Lockheed were allowed to go bankrupt, the American people will lose

31,000 jobs, hundreds of subcontractors would go down in its wake, thousands of Lockheed suppliers would have no options but to declare bankruptcy, and national security would be seriously threatened.

What then is the fix to all of these? The company needed to borrow more money. Not a little. But a lot of it, and because of its financial situation, nobody was willing to lend it money. In the interest of protecting the economy and defending the country, the government had to quickly provide either the money or the credit.

Very quickly, a bailout plan was created by

the Treasury Secretary John B. Connal and the credit was provided. The US government agreed to guarantee the payment of an additional $25 million in loans—an amount which quickly sunk Lockheed deeper into debts by as much as 60%. But, of course that does not make any difference, since the American taxpayer will be made to cosign the account, the banks have no problem with advancing the funds.

What many people don't know about these issues is that this financial mess now provided better motivation for the US government to award as many defense contracts as possible to Lockheed and also ensured that the contracts are as profitable as possible so that the company can stay afloat. This would be an indirect method of paying the banks with tax dollars, but in such a way that it won't raise the suspicion and indignation of the public. This would mean that other defense contractors who have been prudent and ran their business efficiently will now have to suffer a loss of business, but since no one can prove the cause, the argument is dead on arrival even though everyone knows that it is the reality.

Further, this little increase in the defense

expenditure would hardly be noticed by anyone. Seven years later, Lockheed was able to pay back the loan and this was widely hailed as proof that the system and the skill of the players worked.

But on a more careful analysis, two things became quite evident. The first is that Lockheed's operation became highly cost efficient during the period of bailout. Secondly, all the money used in paying back the loans came from defense contracts with the same federal government that was also the one guaranteeing those loans. Under that kind of setup, it does not matter much if the loans were paid back or not. Taxpayers were bound to foot the bill anyway.

CHRYSLER

In 1978, like Lockheed, the Chrysler

Corporation was also teetering on

bankruptcy. It has rolled over its debts to the

banks multiple times, and it was quickly

running out of options. Despite the fact that

O.P.E.C. embargo had increased the cost of

gasoline and people were starting to favor

small import automobiles, the company still

kept on producing cars that were gas-

guzzlers.

Now, it was faced with a problem of selling

a large inventory of cars that nobody wanted

and the debts that has been acquired to build those cars. The timing was another issue. The country was also facing the problem of high interest rates coupled with the fact that the US military was becoming heavily involved in Cambodia; a situation that has led to the crash of the stock market. Banks felt the credit crunch deeply and were even themselves trying their best to keep cash flow steady enough to stay in business. Chrysler needed additional money. It was sink or swim. The company not only needed money to pay off the interest on the loans it had borrowed, it needed money to do other things. To ensure that things fall into place, it wanted more than $1 billion in new capital. In the economic situation at that time, the banks were out of options on how to create anything remotely close to the capital needed by Chrysler.

For their own benefit, managers, bankers, and union leaders found a reason to unite as lobbyists in Washington, D.C.. The American family became the cover for their union. If one of the biggest corporations in America was allowed to close up shop, what would happen to thousands of American families who have breadwinners working in

Chrysler? The shockwave of unemployment. The loss of competition in the auto market.

Well, no one could blame the US congress for not wanting to sink many American families into poverty. Therefore, the US Congress passed a bill allowing the government to guarantee up to $1.5 billion in new loans to Chrysler.

The banks agreed to write down $600 million of their old loans and to exchange an additional $700 million for preferred stock. Both of these moves were advertised as evidence the banks were taking a terrible loss but were willing to yield in order to save the nation.

It should be noted, however, that the value of the stock which was exchanged for previously uncollectable debt rose drastically after the settlement was announced to the public. Furthermore, the new payment not only ensured that the banks continued to get their interest on the old loans made by Chrysler, but the banks also negotiated a replacement of the previous loans with fresh loans. Loans which were of superior quality because they were fully guaranteed by the taxpayers.

This guarantee was so valuable that

Chrysler, despite its previously poor debt performance was able to get loans at 10.35% interest while Ford, which was its more solvent competitor, had to pay a higher interest on its loans at 13.5%. The difference, 3.5%, may not be much on the surface but when applied to the $1.5 billion dollars with a declining balance that will continue for only six years, savings in excess of $165 million is quickly seen, and this is only a modest estimate of the actual size. The real value of this is far bigger than this because without it, the corporation would not have existed, and the banks would have taken a loss of almost their entire loan

exposure.

NEW YORK CITY

Even though the government of the city of New York is a corporation unlike Lockheed and Chrysler, it functions in a considerably similar way to them. One of those ways is debt. In 1975, the city of New York was teetering towards a precipice as it neared the end of its credit line. It became so bad that making its payroll started to become an issue. The reason for this was not supernatural. Neither was it mysterious. In fact, it was quite simple.

New York has long positioned itself as a

welfare state, and success in the political

sphere can only be achieved through

promises of creating programs and subsidies

that are of benefit to the poor. Consequently,

the city became quite notorious for

corruption in the political circle.

Bureaucratic frauds became the order of the

day as the average city was employing an

average of 30 people per 1000 residents. The

salaries of government employees were

vastly higher from what their counterparts

earn in the private sector. While a nurse in a

private hospital earned about $180 per week,

a porter working for the government was

earning $205 for the same hours of work. A

bank teller was earning $154 per week,

while a change maker on the city train

station was earning $212. That is not to even

mention the fact that fringe benefits from

working for the city were double that in the

private industry within the same state. And

there is also the additional cost of free

college education, subsidized housing for

residents, free health care, and a lot of

welfare programs. But the taxes generated

by the city were unable to cover all of this.

Even after the transfer payments by Albany

and Washington added federal and state

taxes to all the confusion, expenses still
outweighed income.

By this time, the state had only three
choices: increases taxes further, cut
expenses, or sink into debt. No one really
though hard and long about the choice. By
1975, the government of New York has
floated so many bonds that it had saturated
the market and could not find anyone that
was willing to lend it money. Out of all of
these debts, a small group of banks owed $2
billion. Chase Manhattan and Citicorp led
this group. When interest could not be paid
any longer on these loans, the banks thought

it was high time they started taking serious action. The bankers and the city officials travelled all the way to Washington, D.C. to plead their case before the people through the US Congress. The largest city in the world cannot be watched as it sinks into bankruptcy, they pleaded. Inability to pay debts will mean that essential and important services would be stopped and millions of New Yorkers would lose services such as garbage removal, transportation, and even security protection. Hunger, disease, crime would be the new order of the day. New York would be a disgrace to the nation. It will be an eyesore and will make a mockery

of the US government.

David Rockefeller at Chase Manhattan,

talked to his friend Helmut Schmidt, the

Chancellor of West Germany, to make a

statement that if New York was left alone, it

will cause a crisis in the international

financial market. Of course, no one wanted

that. Congress could not bear the disgrace it

would pose to the United States as it would

transform the biggest city in the country into

a place of anarchy and chaos. Again, they

also didn't want to cause an international

financial panic that may affect the entire

country.

Therefore, in December 1975, the US Congress had no option other than to pass a bill that authorized the Treasury to make a $2.3 billion loan available to New York City; a loan which is more than twice its debt to other banks. As expected, the city started to pay back interest on previous debts. But first, all of this money would have to be borrowed by Congress because Congress itself is in debt. Again, most of this money would be created, directly or indirectly by the Federal Reserve System. That money would be taken from taxpayer by the loss of purchasing power called inflation, but who cares? Only the banks as the banks make more profits the more money they lend.

As expected there were several restrictions attached to this loan including the implementation of an austerity program and systematic payment schedule. None of which were honored. This is one of the reasons the state will never get out of debt.

Most of the money that the government uses for these bailout does not come from taxes. Almost everything comes from the Federal Reserve System. When this newly created money is given to the banks, it moves out again quickly into the economy where it is mixed and diluted with the money already there. The result of this is the appearance of increasing price, but in reality, what is happening is a reduction in the value of the dollar, with the American people not knowing that they are the one footing the bill. They know that something is not right, but they think it is the local businessman who is trying to be greedy or the farmer who is unnecessarily raising the price of his products. They do not actually understand that these people are also the victims of a monetary system whose value has been eroded by and through the Federal Reserve System.

Since government often guarantees large, corporate loans, one might be tempted to think that the banks which make these loans would not encounter any problem. The truth is that many of them still become insolvent. In fact, insolvency is inherent in the system, a system known as fractional-reserve banking. Regardless of this, a bank can operate in insolvency inasmuch as customers don't know it. But when customers become aware and decide to withdraw their money, for whatever reason, then there would be panic. Now, there is not enough money to go around, which means there is chaos. The ideal solution would have been to compel banks to make good on their promise of "payable upon demand". After all no one asked them to use their money to conduct their own business.

The Federal Reserve System has institutionalized and legalized the dishonesty of issuing more checks than can be fulfilled. It has also created a complex method of disguising this practice as the right way to go about banking. The people are always told that no other way can work. Once that argument is accepted, then all the attention can be channeled into living with this fraud and making it less painful. Based on the assumption that only a small percentage of total depositors will attempt to withdraw at a given time, the Federal Reserve allows the nation's commercial banks to operate with a very thin layer of cash to cover their promise to pay "on demand".

When the bank eventually runs out of money and is unable to keep that promise, the Federal Reserve becomes a discount lender of last resort. But there are often limits to the extent to which this works. Even the Fed in the end will not support a bank that is so in debt it has no realistic way of getting out of it. When the bookkeeping assets of a bank becomes less than its liabilities, the bank owners will then find a way to transfer the losses to the depositors themselves. This would mean the people pay twice; the first time as taxpayers and then as depositors. The vehicle for the achievement of this is the Federal Deposit Insurance Corporation (F.D.I.C.).

The role of the F.D.I.C. is to guarantee that every insured deposit must be paid back regardless of the bank's financial condition. The money to achieve this special function comes from funds which are sourced from assessments against participating banks. Of course, the banks are not really the ones paying this assessment. As with all their expenses, the majority of the cost is shifted to the customer in the form of higher service fees, inflated loan interest rates, and reduced interest rate on deposits.

Normally, the F.D.I.C. is advertised to the people as an insurance fund, but that is just plain deceptive. One of the most important conditions of insurance is what is called "moral hazard". This is a situation in which the holder of an insurance policy has little incentive to avoid or prevent that thing which it is being insured against. When moral hazard is present, people tend to be careless and the likelihood of that thing which they are insured against tends to actually happen.

Depositors are told that their insured accounts are safe even if their bank becomes insolvent in the end. In order to pay for this protection, each and every bank is assessed a recurring insurance premium based on specific percentage of its total deposits. This percentage is the same for every bank and is independent of their previous record or how risky their loans are. In such situations, being cautious does not pay off. The banks who are giving out bad loans make more interest than those ones giving out loans in a conservative fashion. Besides, they are also more likely to get more funds from the F.D.I.C. even though they won't pay more. Conservative banks somewhat feel penalized and therefore become motivated to hand out bad loans to ensure that they are able to keep up with competition and get their "fair

share" of the F.D.I.C. bailout funds. Moral

hazard then becomes inherent in the system.

F.D.I.C. insurance therefore increases the

likelihood of making happen what it is

actually insuring against. The F.D.I.C. is

therefore not the fix to the problem, but a

part of the problem. Responsibility and

accountability are what fix the problem, and

insurance merely removes direct

accountability.

Because the F.D.I.C. has been heavily

polarized by politics, it is embodying the

principle of moral hazard and actually

increases the probability that bank failures will happen. The F.D.I.C. is confronted with three options when it is bailing out a bank which is insolvent.

The first option is payoff. This simply involves paying off the insured depositors and allowing the bank to fall to the mercy of the liquidators. For small banks without any real political strength, this is what becomes of them.

The second option is the "sell off" which involves making arrangement for a bigger bank to assume all the real assets and liabilities of the failing bank at a discount proportional to the risk. In this kind of situation, the banking services are uninterrupted and apart from a change in name, most of the customers are unaware of the transaction. This option is usually available for small and medium banks.

In the two options above, the F.D.I.C. takes control of the bad loans of the failed bank and supplies the money to pay back the insured depositors.

The third option is what is known as bailout, and is the one which deserves the most attention.

A former director of F.D.I.C., Irvine Sprague explains that, "In a bailout, the bank does not close, and everyone—insured or not—is fully protected...Such privileged treatment is accorded by F.D.I.C. only rarely to an elect few."

The elect few the former director was referring to are the large banks. It is only when the number of dollars at risk becomes mind-boggling that that the bailout will then be camouflaged as protection of the public.

Sprague continued:

"The F.D.I.C. Act gives the F.D.I.C. board

sole discretion to prevent a bank from failing, at whatever cost. The board need only make the finding that the insured bank is in danger of failing and 'is essential to provide adequate banking service in its community'..."

Because of this, the F.D.I.C. boards have been perpetually reluctant to make an essentiality finding unless they see that there is a clear and present danger to the nation's financial system.

On many levels, bias towards the large banks is obvious. One of them is the fact that in a bailout, the F.D.I.C. covers all deposits, whether they are insured or not. This is important because the banks pay an assessment based only on their insured deposits. Therefore, if the uninsured deposits are covered also, then that means that the coverage is provided by someone else or it is free.

But what deposits are uninsured? Those in excess of $100,000 and those that are held outside the United States. Which banks hold the majority of these deposits? The large ones, especially those who are operating overseas.

The point at the end of the day is that the big

banks get a free ride when they are bailed out. Their uninsured accounts are paid by the F.D.I.C. and the cost of that coverage is shared by smaller banks and taxpayers. This is not a glitch in operations, but the original way the system was designed to give an advantage to the large banks.

A good solution would be for a voluntary, private insurance program to act as a regulator of the entire banking industry as that would be more honest and effective than the current political scheme in place. Unfortunately, that is not the world we are living in today. The F.D.I.C. does not offer any real protection. It is nothing more than a scheme to bail out the influential members of the banking cartel when they encounter financial difficulty.

As we have already observed, the first step in the line of defense of these bank owners is to have large, defaulted loans restored by the Congress through taxpayer's money. Should that fail with the bank no longer able to conceal its failure through creative bookkeeping, it is almost certain that depositors will rush to collect their money. Money which the bank does not have.

The second line of defense is to have the

F.D.I.C. step into the matter and make those payments for them. Bankers, however, typically don't want this to happen, so it is therefore the last line of action. The reason is because, if this happens, the bank's management will have to be relieved of their duties and another bank will have to take over what is left of the failed bank. When this happens, the stock price will fall drastically, but only small stockholders will be affected. Those who have controlling interest and those in management will know ahead what is going to happen and will sell off the bulk of their shares while the price is still high. The people who started the

problem will not suffer the consequences of

the actions they took. The rich insiders at

the top get richer, and the poor mushrooms

kept in the dark at the bottom get poorer.

The F.D.I.C. will never get adequate funding

to cover the potential liability of the banking

system. If such amount were to exist, the

banks will hold on to it themselves and there

won't even be a need for an insurance fund

in the first place. Instead, the F.D.I.C.

operates on the same assumption as the

banks: the assumption that only a small

percentage of depositors will need their money at a particular point in time. Therefore, the amount of money in the reserve is not usually more than a few percentage points of the entire liability. By law, that percentage, the reserve ratio, is usually 10 percent.

Again, the ledger may show that millions or even billions are in the fund, but that is creative bookkeeping. By law, the money realized from bank assessment must be invested in Treasury bonds, which means it is loaned to the government and spent by the US Congress immediately. In the final stage of this process, therefore, the F.D.I.C. itself will run out of money and turn, first of all to the US Treasury, before turning to the Congress for assistance. In reality, this step is an act of desperation, but through media propaganda, it will be advertised as if that were a strength.

To the people who don't really know what is happening, they think this is something good. But they do not know that Congress, which is already in debt, has no money too. It will not dare to raise taxes openly for the shortfall. Therefore, what it will do is apply for an additional loan by offering more

Treasury bonds for sale. The unsuspecting public picks up and a portion of these IOUs and the Federal Reserve buys up the rest. Peradventure, should there be a monetary crisis at hand and the size of the loan is large, the Fed will again pick up the entire issue. But again, the Fed has no money, so it fabricates an amount of brand new money equal to the IOUs out of nothing and the F.D.I.C. becomes funded.

This new money floods the banks where it is used to pay off depositors. From there, it floods the economy by diluting the value of all money and causing prices to rise. The old paycheck doesn't buy as much in the market any longer, so the people learn to do more with less.

6

THE FEDS TAKE THE GAME OUT OF THE U.S., AT AMERICANS' EXPENSE

It has been previously said that commercial

banks prefer to loan money to big

corporations more than the average small

business owner because they can issue out

huge loans which translate to huge profit. It

has also been said that the banks prefer to

loan out huge sums of money to developing countries since they know that these loans will never be paid back and they can continue earning interest on this loan.

When these countries are unable to pay off these huge loans and the resulting interest, they then make more loans available to these defaulters so that they can continue to pay off the interest on the original loan. Its almost like a drug pusher trying to increase consumption of his addict users. To be able to do this efficiently, they employ the US Congress and Federal Reserve. The Congress will tell the American people that they are trying to save them and their families from unemployment by bailing out the banks. The government calls this "development loans" and the I.M.F. and World Bank are brought in to act as players and referees. This means that these governments are now able to pay off the interest on previous loans with enough left to achieve other political goals.

Soon enough, the recipient country uses up this fresh supply of money and goes back to square one as it no longer has money to service its loans. But this time around, the World Bank and the central banks of these industrialized nations step in to guarantee these loans. Now that the World Bank has taken away this risk of default, the commercial banks will then agree to reduce the interest rate as initially anticipated. The debtor government will then continue to pay its debt.

To ensure that this move is continuous and this government continues to pay loans perpetually, the I.M.F. uses the money from all the citizens of its member nations for this plan. As expected, the chief financiers of the I.M.F. and World Bank are the wealthy, industrialized nations whose wealth will be further reduced, and consequently an epic fall in the standard of living.

The covered-up reality behind all these "development loans" is that America and many other developed countries are subverted by these loans. This is not an accident in any way, but part of the major plan.

A strong nation is least likely to surrender its sovereignty. Americans cannot entertain the thought of turning over their monetary system, military, or courts to a world body consisting of governments which do not have concern for their own people, and have even been despotic towards them. But if Americans can be made to suffer to the point of a collapse in economy and breakdown in civil order, the situation of things will be different. They will be much more likely to give up sovereignty for assistance in the guise of an artificial or "manufactured" emergency.

This is the case with underdeveloped nations as they are not healthy economically. What happens in their case is that their leaders get increasingly addicted to the I.M.F. cash flow that they are unable to break their borrowing habit. These countries are conquered by money instead of arms and ammunition, and

soon enough, they tend to not be truly

independent.

7

HISTORICAL EXAMPLES OF HOW THE FEDS TAKE THE GAME OUT OF THE U.S., AT AMERICANS' EXPENSE

MEXICO

By the first quarter of 1982, almost all

developing countries were struggling to

service their loans. Mexico made its inability to pay on its $85 billion debt public. The Governor of the US Federal Reserve at the time Henry Wallich quickly headed to Switzerland over the issue in order to negotiate with I.M.F. a loan of $4.5 billion through the Bank of International Settlements. The central banks of Europe provided about 40% of the loan equal to $1.85 billion. The rest of that came from the Federal Reserve. The commercial banks decided to postpone payments on the principal for two years before, but with the new loans payment on interest was resumed.

But that didn't solve Mexico's problem.

After a few years, Mexico was running behind on its payment again. In 1985, the banks agreed to postpone $2.9 billion in payments and also postpone another $20 billion, meaning that the banks issued new loans to ensure that interest can be paid on the old ones.

In that same 1985, the then Secretary of the Treasury, James Baker made public the plans of the government to solve the world's debt crisis. The statement encouraged banks to lend to developing countries provided that they promise to put in place economic reforms that will ensure a free market.

This was more talk than an actual plan because there was no real evidence that the government receiving these loans will actually hold their own end of the bargain. Behind the announcement was the idea that the Federal Government using the Federal Reserve System could be counted upon to intervene should things go bad.

Baker advocated for the channeling of $29 billion over three years majorly to Latin America with Mexico being the biggest recipient.

So, it happened that just a few years after the government of Mexico had loaned $55 million to Fidel Castro, it made the announcement that it will only pay what it has and no more. Very quickly, Paul Volcker, who was the head of the Federal Reserve met with the Finance Minister of Mexico, Jesus Silva Herzog and offered American taxpayer's money for Mexico's use.

After that a $600 million short-term loan was further extended to enable Mexico survive its election date fixed for July 4.

This was called a "currency swap" because Mexico exchanged an equal number of pesos which it promised to redeem in US dollars. As everyone knows, Pesos, are worthless in the international markets and it is primarily the reason Mexico needed the American dollars in the first place. The importance of this is not even the sheer size nor the manner of repayment, but the manner in which the loan was made.

First of all, the loan was made by the Federal Reserve directly. The Federal Reserve acted like a central bank for Mexico, not the US. Secondly, the deal was made in almost complete secrecy. William Greider explains how it all went down.

"The currency swaps had another advantage: they could be done secretly. Volcker discreetly informed both the Administration and the key congressional chairmen, and none objected. But the public reporting of currency swaps was required only every quarter, so the emergency loan from the Fed would not be disclosed for three or four months...By that time, Volcker hoped, Mexico would be arranging more substantial new financing from the IMF...The foreign assistance was done as

discreetly as possible to avoid setting off a

panic, but also to avoid domestic political

controversy...Bailing out Mexico, it seemed,

was too grave to be controversial."

As expected, the currency swap didn't solve

the Mexican money problem. So, in 1988,

all the concerned parties decided to

implement another trick called a debt swap.

A debt swap is similar to a currency swap in

that the US government another gives out

something really valuable for something

really worthless. But instead of exchanging

currencies, government bonds are

exchanged. The transaction is made more complex by the time-value of those bonds.

Currencies are valued by their immediate worth, their present purchasing power, while bonds are valued by their future worth; what they can purchase in the future. After the differential factor is made, the process is more or less the same. In this case, Mexico using US dollars bought $492 million worth of American Treasury bonds that pay no interest but will pay $3.67 billion when they become mature in 20 years. Then, Mexico issued its own bonds with the US securities being used as a collateral. This meant that the future value of Mexico's bonds which were considered worthless before, were now guaranteed by the US government. The banks readily changed their old loans for these new Mexicans bonds at a very crazy rate. For instance, $100 million in bonds were accepted in return for cancelling $140 million in old debt. Of course, that resulted in a loss in terms of reduced interest payment, but they were happy to do it because they have been able to change their worthless loans for fully-guaranteed loans.

The press hailed it as a superb monetary

strategy. The Mexican government will be saved more than $200 million in the form of annual interest charges. This will restore cash flow to the banks; and of course, the American taxpayers were told it would cost nothing to them because the Treasury bonds were sold at the normal market rates. The government of Mexico paid for them at the normal rate everyone was paying which is true. But no one mentioned where Mexico got the American dollars it used in buying the bonds.

No one mentioned that the money came through I.M.F. in the form of "foreign-currency exchange reserves." What that means is that these were subsidies from developed nations, most especially the United States. In other words, the US treasury puts up the majority of the money to purchase its own bonds. It sank into debt by about half 500 million and agreed to pay $3.7 billion more in future payments so the Mexican government could go ahead to continuing paying interest to the banks. The official term is bailout, and the American taxpayer bears the brunt.

After the dust had settled in 1989, the US Secretary of State, James Baker and

Treasury Secretary, Nicholas Brady went to
Mexico to get to work on a debt agreement
that would see as I.M.F. as the final
guarantor.

The I.M.F. loaned Mexico $3.5 billion,
which was later increased to $7.5 billion, the
World bank loaned to Mexico another $1.5
billion, and the banks reduced their loan
values by a third. The banks love the idea of
extending new loans and rescheduling the
old. Why wouldn't they? Mexico can now
pay their interest using American taxpayers'
money and those of the Japanese. But of
course, Mexico's problem was not

permanently solved because the economy of

Mexico was suffering from serious inflation

caused by internal debt, in addition to

external debts incurred through borrowing

from the banks.

"Internal debts" and "domestic borrowing"

are euphemisms for the fact that the

government has inflated its supply of money

by selling bonds. The interest the

government must pay to make people buy

those bonds can really be serious and, in

fact, the interest the government of Mexico

was paying on domestic borrowing was

taking away from the economy three times

as much as foreign debt service.

All of these notwithstanding, the chairman of Citicorp, John S. Reed whose bank is one of the biggest lenders in Mexico said that they were ready to lend out even more money. But why is that? The chairman "…believe(d) the Mexican economy is doing well".

By the time 1994 was coming to an end, the game was still being played, and things continued to stay the same. On the 21st of December, the Mexican government went public with the announcement that it no longer had the ability to pay the fixed exchange rate between the peso and the

dollar and that the peso would have to float

in the free market in order to settle at its true

value. The following day the currency

nosedived 39%, and the Mexican stock

market crashed. For sure, the Mexican

government could not pay the interest on its

loans. The following month, US president,

Bill Clinton urged the Congress to approve

US guaranteed loan of up to $40 billion.

The Secretary of the Treasury, Robert Rubin

explained further, *"It is the judgment of all,*

including Chairman Alan Greenspan, that

the probability of the debts being paid [by

Mexico] is exceedingly high."

As Congress was busy deliberating on the issue, Mexico was running out of time. $17 billion to be paid in Mexican bonds will be due in 2 months. This was in January. And by the first of February, $4 billion of that was due. How would the banks get paid? Who would make the payment? This issue cannot be made to wait. On January 31st, President Clinton, acting independently of Congress announced that the US will be handing out a bailout package of over $50 billion in loan guarantees to Mexico. $20 billion of this will come from US Exchange

Stabilization Fund, $17.8 billion will come from the IMF, $10 billion will come from the Bank of International Settlements, and $3 billion from commercial banks.

ARGENTINA

In 1982, Argentina was in trouble. It was unable to make payment to the tune of $2.3 billion. This payment was due in July and August of that same year. The banks extended the loan to Argentina while the I.M.F. made another $2.15 billion available. This enabled Argentina to continue paying the interest on the loan it initially collected and the politicians to have extra money to spend on other things.

Seven months after the new loan was made available, Argentina announced again that it wouldn't be able to make any more payments until the tail-end of 1983. As usual, the banks did not like this because it means they won't be making money. Therefore, they all started making negotiations for rollovers, guarantees, and new I.M.F. loans. The Argentine government then signed an agreement with 350 creditor banks to extend payments on about a fourth of its $13.4 billion debt. The banks agreed to lend an extra $4.2 billion to cover interest payments and political incentives. The I.M.F. stepped in and gave $1.7 billion. The US government stepped in like a big brother and gave an additional $500 million directly. With these new funds, Argentina was then able to pay $850 million in overdue interest to the banks.

By 1988, Argentina was again delinquent and no longer able to make payments on its loans. They were beginning to fall really behind as bankers and politicians gathered together to decide on the next bailout plan.

Again, the payments had to come from the taxpayer's money in the form of new loans, rollovers, and guarantees.

This is what Larry A. Sjaastad at the University of Chicago said:

"There isn't a U.S. bank that would not sell its entire Latin American portfolio for 40 cents on the dollar were it not for the possibility that skillful political lobbying might turn up a sucker willing to pay 50 or 60 or even 90 cents on the dollar. And that sucker is the U.S. Taxpayer."

There are more examples of scenarios where

this is happening, and there is no point repeating it and it's why we will be stopping the case studies here. It could be tiresome to continue to evaluate this in every country. Suffice to say then that this is the same game that the Feds play with Greece, Bolivia, Morocco, Philippines, and many countries of the world.

8

CREATING DEBTS UNDER THE GUISE OF A BANKING SYSTEM

For many Americans, it is quite difficult to come to terms with the fact their total money supply is backed up by nothing else but debts. It is even much more difficult to think that if everyone paid back what was borrowed, then there won't be any money left in existence. Yes, all the money would be returned to the vault of the banks and nothing will be left in anyone's account. Not even a dollar! That is to say, money would cease to exist.

On September 30, 1941, the then Governor of the Federal Reserve System, Marriner Eccles was asked to testified before the House Committee on Banking and Currency. The hearing was aimed at getting information about the role the Federal Reserve played in creating conditions that led to the depression of the 1930s.

The Chairman of the committee, Wright

Patman, asked the Governor how the Fed got the money to buy two billion dollars' worth of government bonds in 1933. The conversation went something like this:

EECCLES: We created it.

PATMAN: Out of what?

ECCLES: Out of the right to issue credit money.

PATMAN: And there is nothing behind it, is there, except our government's credit?

ECCLES: That is what our money system is.

This means that if there were no debts in our money system, then there wouldn't be any money. Of course, some people consider money as an asset, but when it is considered as an aggregate of the total money supply, it is quickly revealed that it is not an asset at all.

Let's illustrate with an example: someone who borrows $1000 may think that he has elevated his financial situation but in fact, that person has not. The $1000 cash received is balanced by the $1000 loan liability, and in the end, the net value is zero.

Bank accounts are more or less like this,

only that the scale is bigger. If one is to add up all the bank accounts in the nation, then one may be tempted to think that all that money means that the economy has a large pool of funds to back it. What is not considered is the fact that all of that money is still owed. Of course, some people will owe nothing. Yet, others will owe many times what they possess. When all is added together, the national balance becomes zero.

In the end, what we consider as money is nothing but an illusion. Debt is the ultimate illusion. In the foreword to the book *100% Money* by Irving Fisher, Robert Hemphill, a former Credit Manager of the Federal Reserve Bank in Atlanta wrote that:

"If all the bank loans were paid, no one could have a bank deposit, and there would not be a dollar of coin or currency in circulation."

This is a staggering thought. We are completely dependent on the commercial banks. Someone has to borrow every dollar we have in circulation, cash, or credit. If the banks create ample synthetic money we are prosperous; if not, we starve. We are absolutely without a permanent money system. When one gets a complete grasp of the picture, the tragic absurdity of our hopeless situation is almost incredible—but there it is.

With the knowledge that money in the US is based on debt, then it should not be surprising then when one discovers that the Federal Reserve System is not concerned about debt reduction, regardless of the fact that it has made public utterances to the contrary. In fact, a publication from the Federal Reserve Bank of Philadelphia reads:

"A large and growing number of analysts, on the other hand, now regard the national debt as something useful, if not an actual

blessing.... [They believe] the national debt need not be reduced at all."

The Federal Reserve Bank of Chicago chips in its own opinion:

"Debt—public and private—is here to stay. It plays an essential role in economic processes... What is required is not the abolition of debt, but its prudent use and intelligent management."

The function of the Federal Reserve System is to convert debt into money. It is very straightforward. First of all, the Fed takes all the government bonds which the public does not buy and writes a check to Congress in exchange for them. The Fed also acquires other debt obligations but government bonds as the biggest in its inventory. Mind you, there is no money to back up all of these debts. This is why fiat dollars are created. By calling these bonds "reserves", the Feds then uses them as the base for creating 9 additional dollars for every dollar created for the bonds themselves.

The government goes ahead to spend the money created for the bonds, whereas the money created on top of those bonds is the source of all the bank loans made to the business and individuals in the country. The result of this is like the creation of money in a printing press, but it is based on accounting gimmicks rather than printing tricks. The issue is that the US Congress and the banking cartel have entered into a kind of relationship in which the cartel has the privilege of collecting interest on money that it creates out of nothing, a continuous override on every single American dollar that is in circulation all over the world.

The U.S. Congress on the other hand has access to unlimited funding without the need to tell citizens that their taxes are being

raised through inflation. The only check on

their ability to borrow and spend is their

credit rating and their tax revenues. As

Uncle's credit rating goes down, the bond

yields go up and the Federal Reserve takes

an ever larger share of the debt as private

creditors flee a bad debtor. A good sign of

the health of the system is the percentage of

new government bonds bought by the Fed.

The greater the percentage, the more

insolvent the government is becoming.

When the percentage is really high, you

know the country is near financial

meltdown.

Because of the fact that the Federal Reserve can be relied upon to convert almost any amount of government debt into money, and because increasing the supply of money leads to inflation, it is very easy to jump into the conclusion that Federal debts and inflation are but two aspects of the same phenomenon. This, however is not always the case. It is very possible to have one or the other.

The Fed banking cartel holds a monopoly in

the manufacture of money. As a result, money is made only when IOUs are "monetized" by the Fed or by commercial banks. When individuals, big corporations, or institutions buy government bonds, they have to use the money they have previously made and saved. That is to say, no new money is created, because they are using money that has already been in existence.

Therefore, the sale of government bonds to the Fed banks cause inflation, but when it is sold to the private sector, it does not cause such a problem. This is the primary reason the US avoided serious inflation in the

1980s when the federal government was getting deeper into debt than ever in its previous history. By keeping the rate of interest high on government bonds, private investors were attracted, including those in other countries. Very little new money was created because most of the bonds were purchased with the American dollars that are already in existence. This, of course, was only a temporary fix in the best scenario. As we progress to the present, those bonds are maturing perpetually and are being replaced by still a plethora of new bonds that include both the original debt plus accumulated interest.

Eventually, at the end of the day, the process must come to an end. The Ponzi scheme will have to implode. When this happens, the Fed will have no other choice but to literally buy back all the debt of the '80s—that means that it will have to replace all of the formerly invested private money with newly manufactured fiat money—and even more to cover the interest, causing massive inflation.

On the other hand, the Federal Reserve has the option of manufacturing money even if the federal government does not sink deeper into debt. For instance, the huge increase in the supply of money leading up the crash of the stock market in 1929 happened at a time when the national debt was being gradually paid off. Every year, from 1920 through 1930, federal revenue was bigger than expenses, and there were relatively few government bonds available for purchase. The serious inflation of the supply of money was made possible by the conversion of commercial bank loans into "reserves" at the Fed's discount window and by the Fed's purchase of banker's acceptances, which are commercial contracts for the purchase of goods.

Now, the options are even bigger. With the Monetary Control Act of 1980, it is even more possible for the Federal Reserve to monetize almost any debt instrument, including IOUs from foreign governments. The clear purpose of this act is to make sure that it is possible to bail out those governments that are finding it difficult to pay their interest on loans received from American banks. When the Fed creates fiat American dollars to give foreign governments in exchange for their worthless bonds, the money path is a little bit longer and more twisted, but the effect is almost similar to the purchase of US Treasury Bonds. The newly created dollars go to the foreign governments, then to the American banks where they become cash reserves.

At the end of the day, they flow back into the US money pool (multiplied by nine) in the form of additional loans. The cost of all of these will once again be carried by the American citizen through the loss of purchasing power. Expansion of the money supply, and the consequent inflation that follows no longer require federal deficits.

As long as there is somebody willing to borrow American dollars, the cartel will have the opportunity to create those dollars specifically for the purpose of purchasing their bonds, and by so doing, expanding their money supply.

It is important not to forget that one of the chief reasons the Fed was created was so that it will be possible for congress to spend money without the public knowing that it was being taxed for it.

The people have shown time and time again their indifference to this rip-off. Therefore, at the moment, the relationship between the banking cartel and the politicians is still expected to continue, unchanged. Therefore, even though the Fed may also create fiat money in place of commercial debts and for bonds of foreign government, its major concern will be to continue supplying Congress. The result of this troubles the mind. Since the supply of money at the moment is related to national debt, therefore paying off that debt would cause the money to disappear. Even reducing the debt would cripple the economy. Therefore, as long as the Federal Reserve exists, the country will perpetually be in debt. The purchase of bonds from the government of other countries is increasing in the current political climate. Our own supply of money is based on their debts, and even if they are able to pay it off, they won't be allowed to.

Many Americans don't know that inflation is a tax. As the system currently stands it is a top down system that is the most unfair of all taxes because it is falls heavily those at the bottom, the 99 %, who are able to leverage money the least. That means the poorest of the people on fixed incomes, and the middle and low-income earners. What is important is that without fiat money, this tax would be impossible. But fiat money in the US is created by the Federal Reserve

System. Therefore, it would still be accurate to say that the Federal Reserve System generates the most unfair methods of taxation.

If money was distributed evenly among all the citizens then this would not be the case, but in a system where the wealthiest get to use all of the money first before inflation hits it leaves those with less money no way to equal the playing field. Hence, the real inflation adjusted purchasing power of the average family income has steadily gone down over the years and the average American has become poorer due to the inflation rate exceeing the wage increase rate.

The people who authorize the process of monetizing debts and the people who do it know for sure that it is not true debt. It is not true debt as no one in government expects it to be paid back—ever. The reason for all of this is to make sure that that politicians have free spending money without the stress involved in raising taxes directly, and also to ensure that the banking cartel has access to continuous supply of money. But these people are only looking out for themselves.

If this is so, it begs the question: why does

the federal government even bother with taxes? Why can't it just operate on the debts that it has monetized? The reason for this is twofold.

First of all, if the government did, people would have to start asking questions about the source of the money, and they may wake up one day to realize that inflation is a tax. Thus, open taxes at a certain level serve to perpetuate public ignorance which is very important to the success of the commercial scheme. The second reason is that taxes, particularly the progressive ones, are tools used by elitist social planners to limit the middle class.

Again, one of the myths of the Federal
Reserve is the argument that it is needed to
stabilize the economy, yet, it has achieved
the reverse. In the years before each Crash
of 1929, destabilization was evident, but the
same cause-and-effect still remain even
today. As long as men are given the
opportunity to influence the supply of
money, they will always want to circumvent
the natural laws of demand and supply. No
matter how good their intentions or motive
is, they will cause disruption in the natural

flow of things. Now when these disruptions are becoming obvious, they will alter that by switching in the opposite direction. But before these actions are taken, there will already be new forces at work which the players will be unable to perceive until manifested.

The following paint a better picture of the market crash and rise will make it clearer why the Federal Reserve destabilizes the economy:

Between 1920 and 1929, there were three distinct business cycles with a lot of minor ones within them. For the average

American, it was confusing and destructive. For the investor, it was more like a roller-coaster ride to nowhere.

UP: The Fed had inflated the money supply to pay for World War I. The resulting boom caused prices to rise.

DOWN: In 1920, the Fed raised interest rates to reduce the inflation which caused a recession, and prices tumbled. Farmers were hit the hardest, and hundreds of country banks were closed.

UP: In 1921, the Fed reduced interest rates to stop the recession and to help the governments of Europe. Inflation and expanding debt resulted.

DOWN: In 1923, the Fed tightened credit to curb inflation.

UP: But that was offset by its simultaneous policy of lowering the rate at the discount window, thus encouraging banks to borrow new reserves to expand the money supply.

UP: In 1924, the Fed created $500 million dollars in new money. Within a year, the commercial banks increased that into more than $ 4 billion, an expansion of eight-to-one. The boom that followed took on the character of speculation rather than investment. Prices in the stock market rose drastically.

DOWN: In 1926, the Florida land boom collapsed, and the economy began to contract once again.

UP: In 1927, Montagu Norman of the Bank of England paid a visit to the US to consult with Benjamin Strong. Not too long after his visit, the Fed pumped new money into the system, and the boom returned.

DOWN: In the spring of 1928, the Fed contracted credit to stop the boom.

UP: But the banks shifted their reserves into time deposits (where customers agree to wait before withdrawing their money). Since time deposits require a smaller reserve ratio than demand deposits, it give the bank the opportunity to issue more loans than before. That offset the Fed's contraction of credit.

UP: By that time, the British government had used up its previous subsidy which was used to maintain its welfare state. Early 1928, the pound sterling was again falling on the international market, and gold began to flow back into the US. Once again, the Federal Reserve came to aid of the Bank of

England, the bank it was modeled after. The Fed bought a huge volume of banker's acceptances to depress interest rates and halt the flow of gold. The money supply suddenly increased by almost $2 billion.

DOWN: In August, the Fed reversed its expansionist policy by selling Treasury bonds in the open market and raising interest rates. The money supply began to contract. It was the final bubble.

9

FAILING TO SUCCESS

Towards the end of WWII, the major world leaders met in Bretton Woods as it was obvious that the allies were on the verge of winning the war. Thus, an agreement was reached to make the US Dollars the global currency and Roosevelt promised the US would not overproduce her currency. Also, it was agreed that an ounce of gold would be exchangeable for $35. Thus, the British Pound lost her status as the global currency and the Bank of England was nationalized. The Federal Reserve overproduced the Dollars as expected and caused economic problems for the world. France realized the plot decided to pull out of the deal and decided to exercise her option to trade ounces of gold for her dollar reserves. The US Government knowing they had inadequate gold to trade suspended the gold convertibility of the US Federal Reserve

Notes. This move ended the Bretton Woods agreement.

Nations became skeptical about trading with the United States once they realized the country didn't have enough gold reserve. To pacify them, President Richard Nixon pledged US Lands and Natural reserves as collateral without any concern for the American people who own the land. Also, the US made a deal with Middle Eastern nations to trade Arab oil in dollars rather than respective local currencies and thus moving to petrodollar i.e. dollar was backed by oil. The agreement also included the Arab countries investing in the US Economy but by then, the US had nothing much to offer apart from Real Estate. European Industrial output was superior while American foods were unwanted. Iraq wanted out of the deal and as a result, America attacked Saddam Hussein under the guise of Iraq keeping nuclear weapons which have not been found to this day.

Muammar Gaddafi was also attacked because he decided to change Libya's oil currency from US Dollars to Gold Dinars. French President, Nicolas Sarkozy, labelled him a threat to the financial security of the world.

After his death, Libya is back to the Dollar exchange and the nation is in economic woes. All the countries attacked by the United States of America are not members of the Bank for International Settlement and as such run their economic affairs independently.

Recently, the German Government have asked the New York Federal Reserve and Bank of France to return some of German's gold bullion. Both countries have asked for a considerable amount of time to return the reserve which shows they have used it for other endeavors. France is also planning to attack Mali, a nation with vast gold reserve under the guise of attacking Al-Qaeda. What a coincidence.

The United States claims to export democracy and fundamental human rights to those "conquered" countries but the state of those countries after US invasion has been really terrible. The perceived clash of ideologies is just a narrative to give the Private Central Banks the needed opportunity to make profit at the expense of the average person. Islam forbids the lending of money at an interest rate which is against the plan of the Private Bankers. As such, the attack against Radical Terrorism is at best an attack on Islam and its beliefs.

In the end, it is obvious that the private central banks create a form of obligation (debt) payable to the Private Central Banks. Thus, they are creating a form of enslavement against the people. Private Central Bank and their agents are currently attempting to take over Ukraine using their ploys but the Russian Government is currently in her way by offering a better deal to the Ukrainians. The uprising in Ukraine was sponsored by the Private banks in order to to take over the country's economic affairs.

China is also a target because rapidly

developing nations under the acronym 'BRICS' i.e. Brazil, Russia, India, China and Singapore as these countries and about 80 others want to make the Chinese currency, the Yuan, their official international trading currency. The end game is to cause a war between North Korea and China which would be to their advantage.

Everyone should know this; the Private Central Banks do not care about anyone else but their own interest. As long as they exist, strife, war, pestilence and economic problems will continue to abound in the world.

The solution is to abolish Private Central Banks all over the world. Only then can peace and prosperity reign.

"Banks do not have an obligation to promote the public good." -- Alexander Dielius, CEO, Germany, Austrian, Eastern Europe Goldman Sachs, 2010

"I am just a banker doing God's work." -- Lloyd Blankfein, CEO, Goldman Sachs, 2009

10

CONCLUSION

Although, all of these monetary strategies and policies may appear mysterious and complicated to the untrained eye, the truth is that they are governed by well-established rules which all the players (bankers and politicians) strictly follow.

The most important thing to note in all of this is that the money in the banking system has been created out of nothing through the process of making loans. In fact, a defaulted loan is of little value to the bank, but only shows up on the ledger as a reduction is assets without a corresponding reduction in liabilities. But if the bad loans become bigger than the assets, then the bank will become insolvent in the technical sense and will have to close its doors to business.

Therefore, the first step in ensuring that such a bank survives is to do everything it can do to not write off these large, bad loans and, if possible continue to receive payments of interest on them.

In order to avoid default on bad loans, the endangered loans will need to be rolled over and increased. By so doing, the borrower has more money to continue to pay interest on the old loans and has new money to spend. Its like paying your Mastercard with your Visa Card: A juggling act at best to delay an inevitable calamity. But of course, the original problem has not been solved, it is merely extended, deferred and worsened. The metaphorical can is kicked down the road.

After a while, the banking cartel will have no other choice but to bring in the Federal Government to guarantee the payment of these loans in the event that the borrower fails to pay their debts in future. The Cartel will try hard to convince the US Congress that not guaranteeing the payment will result in hardship and great economic depression for the American people. When the Congress agrees, then the burden of the loan is transferred from the bank's books to the necks of the taxpayer.

In the event that the US Congress disagrees and the bank faces insolvency, then it will have no other choice than to ask the F.D.I.C.

to pay off its depositors. But the F.D.I.C. is

not a real insurance because it increases the

likelihood of making happen the thing which

it is supposed to prevent from happening. A

part of the F.D.I.C. funds are obtained from

assessment against the banks. But in the end,

they are paid for by the depositors

themselves. When these funds run out, the

Federal Reserve is brought into the equation

to create fresh new money. This money

floods the economy creating the appearance

of a rise in the cost of goods and services,

but which in reality is a fall in the value of

the dollar. The eventual cost of the bailout,

therefore is still paid by the people through

inflation—a hidden tax.

As BC Forbes, who later became the

founder of Forbes Magazine, wrote in

Leslie's Weekly in 1916:

"Picture a party of the nation's greatest

bankers stealing out of New York on a

private railroad car under cover of darkness

, stealthily hiking hundreds of miles South,

embarking on a mysterious launch, sneaking

on to an island deserted by all but a few

servants, living there a full week under such

rigid secrecy that the names of not one of

them was once mentioned lest the servants

learn the identity and disclose to the world

this strangest, most secret expedition in the

history of American finance."

A mental picture of such secrecy can only

show the extreme measures that were

necessary to perpetrate a deception on such

a large scale.

Through the heinous system created by

deception the Federal Reserve central bank

was create by a Congress that had no

constitutional authority to do so. Powers not

explicitly granted to Congress by the

Constitution are inherently denied to

Congress under the Tenth Amendment. Never was the authority to establish a central bank granted in the Constitution. In fact, the founding fathers if this nation in drafting of the constitution were explicitly against central banks.

Congress through the swipe of a pen in an act it never had the authority to inflict on the American people ceded total control over the value of our money to a secretive central bank.

Today the dollar is worth only four cents compared to the purchasing power of a dollar of 1913 when the Federal Reserve was created.

Paper currencies have and maintain no

intrinsic value and eventually are all doomed to collapse. History abounds with examples of suffering caused by such needless and inevitable collapses. These collapses always effect a nation's poor and middle class the most.

The monetary system at its core is designed to transfer wealth from the poor and middle class to the privileged rich. Even worse, it makes their reckless gambling loss into profit for them, as it is Insured with the people's money. Even when they royally screw up (2008) they still have no consequences.

While Congress congratulates itself for raising the minimum wage by mandate, in reality they have lowered the standard of living for almost the whole nation by allowing the Federal Reserve to devalue the dollar. Eventually the growing social inequalities created by our monetary system will either lead to collapse or civil war.

Is it any wonder that we went from the richest nation in history to a nation of debtors, like all of the nations before us to tried fiat currency systems? Those who do not learn history are doomed to repeat it.